The Giant's Causeway

Rob Waring, *Series Editor*

HEINLE
CENGAGE Learning

Australia • Brazil • Japan • Korea • Mexico • Singapore • Spain • United Kingdom • United States

Words to Know

This story is set in Northern Ireland. It happens in a place called the 'Giant's Causeway.'

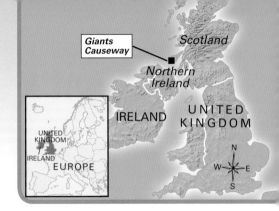

Did a Giant Make the Giant's Causeway? Read the paragraph. Then, complete the sentences with the words in the box.

The Giant's Causeway is a formation made of rock on the Irish coast. There are many legends about who, or what, made it. One story is about a giant called Finn MacCool. According to the story, Finn had a fight with a giant from Scotland. The legend says that Finn MacCool took 40,000 pieces of rock and built a walkway between Northern Ireland and Scotland. People say he did it because he wanted to go to Scotland to find the Scottish giant.

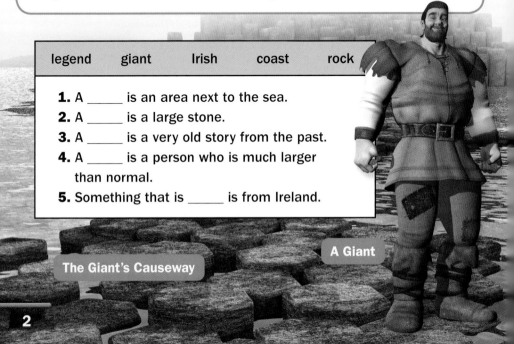

legend	giant	Irish	coast	rock

1. A _____ is an area next to the sea.
2. A _____ is a large stone.
3. A _____ is a very old story from the past.
4. A _____ is a person who is much larger than normal.
5. Something that is _____ is from Ireland.

The Giant's Causeway

A Giant

B Did a Volcano Make the Giant's Causeway? Read the paragraph. Then match each word with the correct definition.

Scientists are people who study the structure and actions of natural things. Scientists, such as geologists, believe that the Giant's Causeway has a more scientific explanation. One idea is that a volcanic eruption made it. When a volcano erupts, it produces lava. The lava becomes dry and hard and can make interesting formations in the rock. Geologists think the Giant's Causeway is a natural rock formation from a volcano.

1. geologists _____

2. volcano _____

3. erupt _____

4. lava _____

5. formation _____

a. explode; blow up

b. scientists that study the earth

c. hot, melted rock

d. a mountain with a hole in the top

e. things that are arranged in a particular way

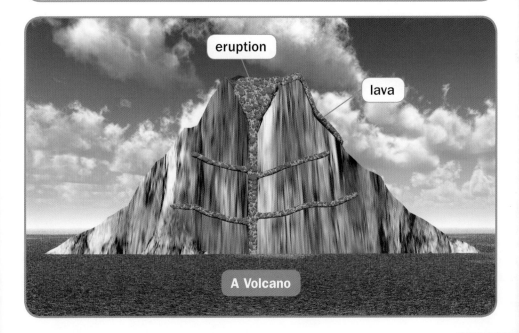

eruption

lava

A Volcano

The stone walkway on the coast of Northern Ireland is one of the country's most important **tourist**[1] centers. It's a special place of science and legends. Many visitors come to the area each year. They want to see the Giant's Causeway, Northern Ireland's first **World Heritage Site**.[2]

---

[1]**tourist:** a visitor who travels for enjoyment
[2]**World Heritage Site:** an important cultural place, chosen by the United Nations Educational, Scientific, and Cultural Organization (UNESCO)

🎧 **CD 3, Track 05**

But where does the Giant's Causeway come from? Why does it exist? People can't agree. There's a big discussion about the beginnings of the walkway. There are people who believe that there is a scientific explanation for it, and there are those who believe in a legend.

For some people, these 40,000 pieces of **basalt**[3] are a natural formation of rock. However, for other people, the Giant's Causeway is the home of an Irish giant named Finn MacCool. But who was he? And why do people say he built the causeway?

---

[3]**basalt:** a kind of rock

In the past, Hill Dick was a **tour guide**[4] for visitors to this beautiful coast. Dick tells the old legend of Finn MacCool. "Finn was one of the great characters in Irish **mythology**[5] or, if you like, Irish fact," says Dick with a smile. He then tells a story about how Finn was angry with a Scottish giant who lived **25 miles**[6] across the sea. So Finn decided to go to Scotland. Finn was not a good swimmer, so he used rocks from volcanoes to build a road to Scotland. He called it the Giant's Causeway.

[4]**tour guide:** a person who shows visitors around and gives them information about a place
[5]**mythology:** stories of people from the past
[6]**25 miles:** 40.2 kilometers

Summarize

Close your book. Retell the story of Finn MacCool. Tell it to a partner or write it in a notebook. Use your own words.

Is the legend of Finn MacCool and his causeway true? Did he really build it so that he could catch the Scottish giant? Well, perhaps—if you use your imagination.

However, not everyone agrees with the legend. Scientists like geologist Patrick McKeever have their own, more scientific, story. They say that a volcano made the Giant's Causeway about 60 million years ago. That was a very long time before humans ever lived in this lovely part of the world.

Some people think a volcano erupted and made the Giant's Causeway.

eruption

What do you think?

1. How does McKeever explain the Giant's Causeway?

2. Does he believe the story of Finn MacCool?

3. What makes you think that way?

McKeever tells about what he thinks made the Giant's Causeway. "The lava that was erupted, was erupted very, very quickly and the flows were very, very thick," he says. He then explains that the lava was a bit like **mud**[7] on a hot day. Mud becomes dry and shrinks, or gets smaller when it dries. McKeever says that a similar condition with the lava made the many-sided **columns**.[8] For McKeever and other geologists, the causeway is a natural rock formation.

---

[7]**mud:** a soft combination of water and earth
[8]**column:** a tall post which is made of stone

lava flow

columns

It was much warmer and there was volcanic activity in Northern Ireland 55 to 65 million years ago.

So was it Finn MacCool or a volcano that made the Giant's Causeway? Maybe it doesn't really matter. Tourists from all over the world have been visiting here, and the nearby Irish coast, since the 1800s. These people don't have to believe in the legend—or the scientific explanation—to want to come to this interesting place.

Hill Dick explains why the area has so many visitors. He claims that every visitor has a personal experience when they look at the rocks and the formations they make. He feels that every visitor can make their own personal story about the place. Each visitor has their own experience at the Giant's Causeway because each visitor can use his or her own imagination. "You can **weave**[9] your own story around it," he says. "You can look at a rock and say, 'That, **reminds**[10] me of something...'[or] 'That looks like something...'"

---

[9]**weave:** create or make
[10]**remind:** make a person think of something or somebody

Year after year, large numbers of tourists and children visit the Giant's Causeway and listen to the legend of Finn MacCool. As they hear these stories, they begin to wonder about the Giant's Causeway… and where it really came from.

Will the legend of Finn MacCool continue? The answer is probably 'yes'. These visitors and their interest may just help the legend of the giant Finn MacCool live for a very long time.

After You Read

1. _____ people come to see the Giant's Causeway every year.
   A. Some
   B. Few
   C. Other
   D. Many

2. Who was Finn MacCool?
   A. a geologist
   B. a giant
   C. a tourist
   D. a tour guide

3. How many pieces of basalt are in the Giant's Causeway?
   A. 40,000
   B. 60 million
   C. 25
   D. 27

4. The word 'used' on page 9 can be replaced by:
   A. dried
   B. made
   C. erupted
   D. moved

5. On page 10, 'he' in paragraph one refers to:
   A. a Scottish giant
   B. Hill Dick
   C. Finn MacCool
   D. a geologist

6. Which is a good heading for page 13?
   A. Wet Mud Makes Columns
   B. Slowly Erupting Lava Turns to Mud
   C. How a Volcano Made the Giant's Causeway
   D. Lava Dries and Shrinks the Mud

7. Geologists think the many-sided columns were made by all of the following ways EXCEPT:
   A. Lava that erupted very quickly.
   B. Wet mud dried on a hot day.
   C. Thick flows of lava.
   D. Lava got smaller while drying.

8. On page 17, the word 'it' refers to:
   A. the causeway
   B. the story
   C. the legend
   D. the science

9. On page 18, the phrase 'tourists and children' can be replaced by:
   A. scientists
   B. tour guides
   C. visitors
   D. geologists

10. The legend of Finn MacCool may last for a very long time because:
   A. The legend is scientific fact.
   B. A lot of children and tourists come to study mythology.
   C. Geologists like to tell the story to tourists.
   D. Visitors like to think about where the causeway came from.

11. The Giant's Causeway is a special place of both _____ and _____.
   A. science, legend
   B. Ireland, Scotland
   C. fact, geologists
   D. story, legend

A Volcano Called VESUVIUS

Herculaneum was a town about five miles south of Naples in Italy. Two thousand years ago, it was a quiet farming center and about five thousand people lived there. It was on the coast and had beautiful views across the sea. In August of the year A.D. 79, everything changed. A nearby volcano called Vesuvius erupted and killed the people in the town. A writer named 'Pliny the Younger' recorded what happened. He was the first person in history ever to describe a volcanic eruption. Because of Pliny's story, Vesuvius is probably the best-known volcano in the world.

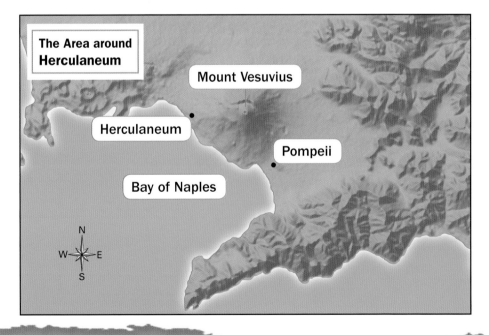

The Area around Herculaneum

Mount Vesuvius

Herculaneum

Pompeii

Bay of Naples

N
W—E
S

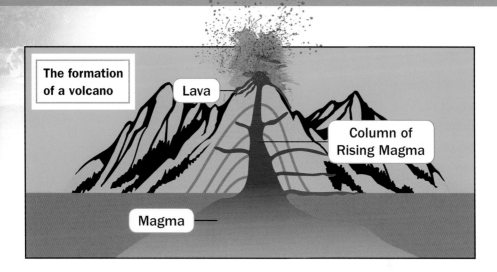

The formation of a volcano

Lava

Column of Rising Magma

Magma

On that August afternoon, most people in the area weren't worried about the volcano. However, suddenly Vesuvius erupted sending hot lava down its sides toward the coast. This lava was fifty feet deep in some places. At the same time, large pieces of rock fell from the volcano. As the hot lava moved quickly toward the town, many people ran to the coast hoping to find safety. However, within four minutes of the first eruption, lava covered the whole town of Herculaneum. Lava also covered the city of Pompeii, a large and important business center nearby.

Scientists now use the term 'Plinean' to describe very fast eruptions like the one that covered Herculaneum. This term comes from the name of Pliny the Younger. Some eruptions are much slower than the one Pliny the Younger described. For example, thousands of tourists visit Hawaii every year to see its quieter volcanoes.

However, it does not matter whether their eruptions are quick or slow, all volcanoes are formed in a similar way. They all begin when magma under the ground starts to move. As it rises, this magma forms a column and then comes out the top of a volcano as lava. Sometimes the lava does not look hot and may move very slowly, but people must always be careful not to get too close.

CD 3, Track 06

Word Count: 312
Time: _____

Vocabulary List

basalt (6)
coast (2, 4, 9, 14)
column (13)
erupt (3, 13)
formation (3, 6, 8, 13, 17)
geologist (3, 10, 13)
giant (2, 3, 4, 6, 9, 10, 12, 13, 14, 17, 18)
Irish (2, 6, 9, 14)
lava (3, 13)
legend (2, 6, 10, 17, 18)
mud (13)
mythology (9)
remind (17)
rock (2, 3, 6, 9, 13, 17)
tour guide (9)
tourist (4, 14, 18)
volcano (3, 9, 10, 14)
weave (17)
World Heritage Site (4)